Festivals through the Year

Autumn

Anita Ganeri

Heinemann LIBRARY

First published in Great Britain by Heinemann Library
Halley Court, Jordan Hill, Oxford OX2 8EJ
a division of Reed Educational and Professional Publishing Ltd.
Heinemann is a registered trademark of Reed Educational & Professional Publishing Limited.

OXFORD MELBOURNE AUCKLAND IBADAN JOHANNESBURG
BLANTYRE GABORONE PORTSMOUTH (NH) USA CHICAGO

Designed by Ken Vail Graphic Design, Cambridge
Illustrations by Pat Murray
Printed by Wing King Tong in Hong Kong

03 02 01 00 99
10 9 8 7 6 5 4 3 2

ISBN 0 431 05458 4

British Library Cataloguing in Publication Data

Ganeri, Anita
Autumn. – (Festivals through the year)
1. Autumn festivals – Great Britain – Juvenile literature
I. Title
394.2'64'0941

Acknowledgements
The Publishers would like to thank the following for permission to reproduce photographs:
Andes Press Agency/Carlos Reyes Manzo, pp. 7, 20, 24, 25, 29; Collections, (Forder, John & Eliza) p. 14, (Shuel, Brian) p. 15, 18, 23 top and below, (Young, Archie), p. 27, (Wender, John), p. 22; Emmett, Phil & Val, pp. 6, 16, 17; Harrison, Graham, p, 21; J. Allan Cash, p. 4; Radovan, Zev, pp. 10, 11; Rex Features, p.26; Sanders, Peter, p. 28; Soester, Julietter, pp. 8, 9, 13; The Stock Market, p.12.

Cover photograph reproduced with permission of Phil and Val Emmett

Our thanks to Peter Woodward, who works with SHAP Working Party on World Religions in Education, for his comments in the preparation of this book.

Every effort has been made to contact copyright holders of any material reproduced in this book. Any omissions will be rectified in subsequent printings if notice is given to the Publisher.

Contents

Words printed in **bold letters like these**
are explained in the Glossary.

Celebrating autumn

As summer ends, autumn begins. The days become shorter and nature prepares for winter. Many trees lose their leaves. But before this happens, they change colour from summer green to brilliant shades of red, russet, orange and gold.

Autumn trees.

Many festivals are held in autumn. Some are festivals of light which ask the Sun to shine for longer. Others mark the start of a new year. Many celebrate the gathering of the harvest before winter begins. Some have special religious meanings, when people remember the lives of their gods or teachers and important times in their religion's history.

Festivals are often happy times with many ways of celebrating. There are special services and ceremonies, delicious food, dancing, cards and gifts. Some festivals are holidays when you have a day off school.

Some festivals happen on the same day each year. Others change from year to year. For festivals that change, you will find a dates circle, which tells you when the festival will be. (The future dates of some festivals are only decided upon nearer the time, so some dates in the circles may be out by a day or two.)

Dates

7 October 1998
26 October 1999
15 October 2000
4 October 2001
6 October 2002

Moon dates

The calendar we use every day has a year of 365 days, divided into 12 months. Most months have 30 or 31 days. Some religions use different calendars which are based on the Moon. A Moon month is the time it takes for the Moon to travel around the Earth. This is about 27 days, which gives a shorter year. So, each year, the Moon calendar falls out of step with the everyday calendar. This is why some festivals fall on different days each year.

Janmashtami

Dates

14 August 1998
2 September 1999
22 August 2000
12 August 2001

Later dates not known

At Janmashtami, in August or September, **Hindus** celebrate the birthday of **Krishna**, the blue god. He is famous for making mischief and playing tricks on his friends. He is also a great hero who helps and looks after people. His birthday is a very joyful time.

Krishna is said to have been born at midnight and Hindus stay up late to welcome him. They decorate the **mandir** with lights and flowers, and listen to stories about Krishna's birth. In pride of place stands a small cradle, covered with a cloth. When midnight comes, the cloth is removed to show an **image** of baby Krishna inside. People rock the cradle and leave gifts of sweets around it.

Rocking the baby Krishna in his cradle

Ganesha Chaturthi

Another happy birthday for **Hindus** is that of **Ganesha**, the elephant-headed god. This is celebrated in August or September, with a festival called Ganesha Chaturthi. Ganesha was the son of the god, **Shiva**, and his wife, Parvati. Hindus pray to Ganesha when they start something new, like a journey, a new school or moving house.

Dates

28 August 1998
13 September 1999
1 September 2000
22 August 2001
Later dates not known

To mark this day, Hindus visit the **mandir** or worship at home. They offer gifts of flower garlands and special sweets, called luddus, to Ganesha.

An **image** of the god Ganesha.

Make a garland

Make a birthday garland to offer to Ganesha from real flower heads or balls of tissue paper. Thread a needle with a long piece of cotton and carefully push the flowers onto it. Take off the needle and tie the ends together.

Rosh Hashanah

The **Jewish** festival of Rosh Hashanah falls in September or October. This is the most important time in the Jewish year. It is the start of the New Year when **Jews** celebrate the creation of the world. It is also the beginning of ten special days, called the Days of **Penitence**. This is a time when Jews say sorry to God for all the bad things they have done in the past year. They promise to learn from their mistakes and to do better in the New Year.

Dates

21 September 1998
11 September 1999
30 September 2000
18 September 2001
7 September 2002

A colourful selection of cards for Rosh Hashanah.

Eating apples and honey at Rosh Hashanah.

Over the two days of Rosh Hashanah, there are special services in the **synagogue**. A musical instrument, called a **shofar**, is blown. It makes a loud, piercing sound like a trumpet and reminds Jews of God's great power. People also send each other cards to wish them 'Leshanah Tovah Tikatev' – Happy New Year!

Apples and honey

At Rosh Hashanah, people eat slices of apple dipped in honey. This is a way of wishing each other a sweet and happy New Year.

Yom Kippur

The tenth Day of **Penitence** after Rosh Hashanah is called Yom Kippur, or the Day of **Atonement**. It is the day on which **Jews** ask God's forgiveness for their wrongs. For Jews, this is the holiest day of the year.

On the day before Yom Kippur, people enjoy a special feast. On Yom Kippur itself, they spend the whole day **fasting**. This means they do not eat or drink anything at all. This is a way of making up for their wrongs. Many Jews spend much of this day in the **synagogue** in worship and thought. They believe that God will forgive them if they are truly sorry.

A Jewish man deep in thought.

Dates

30 September 1998
20 September 1999
9 October 2000
27 September 2001
16 September 2002

At sunset on Yom Kippur, the **shofar** is blown once to mark the end of the fast.

Saying sorry

On the night before Yom Kippur, Jews say sorry to anyone they have quarrelled with. This might be a friend, a relation or a neighbour. Only then can they say sorry properly to God.

Sukkot

In September or October, **Jews** celebrate the festival of Sukkot. They remember the time when their **ancestors** lived in the desert, thousands of years ago. Some lived in tents. Others built huts out of leaves and branches. These huts were called sukkot. They also remember how God looked after the Jews.

During the festival, some Jews build their own sukkah in the garden or at the **synagogue**. Jews eat their meals in the sukkah for the eight or nine days of the festival.

When Jews build a sukkah, they leave the roof open enough to see the sky.

Dates

5 October 1998
25 September 1999
14 October 2000
2 October 2001
22 September 2002

Children holding
Sukkot branches.

There is a special Sukkot service in the synagogue. Everyone holds branches from three trees in their left hands and a citron, a fruit like a large lemon, in their right. They walk around the synagogue seven times, waving the branches. Sukkot is also a harvest festival.

Special plants

Each of the four plants used at Sukkot has a special meaning. The palm branch stands for your backbone. The myrtle is your eyes; the willow your lips and the citron your heart. These plants remind Jews to worship God with their whole bodies.

Harvest Festival

For farmers, autumn was the time for bringing in the crops from the fields. It marked the end of a year's hard work. At that time, most of the farm work was done by hand. When the last stalks of corn were cut, the farmers held a great feast to thank God for a good harvest.

Bringing in the autumn harvest.

Today, **Christians** celebrate Harvest Festival at **church** services on any Sunday in September or October. They sing **hymns** and say prayers to thank God for all his goodness. With them, they take fruit, flowers and vegetables to decorate the church. People also bake special loaves of bread. All the food is later given away. Afterwards, some churches hold a harvest supper.

In some places, by the sea, people also hold festivals to celebrate a good year's fishing.

A church decorated for Harvest Festival.

Corn dollies

People used to make little corn dolls from the last stalks of corn cut at harvest-time. These were hung in the farmhouse kitchen or barn until the new year. Then they were dug back into the soil to bring good luck in the next year's harvest.

Dassehra

The **Hindu** festival of Dassehra falls in September or October. It remembers the story of the god, **Rama**, who rescues his wife, Sita, from **Ravana**, a wicked demon king. This story reminds Hindus that good always wins over evil.

Dates

21 September 1998
27 October 1999
7 October 2000
26 October 2001

Later dates not known

Acting out the story of Rama and Sita.

The story of Rama is told in the Ramayana, one of the Hindus' **holy** books. During Dassehra, it is acted out in a play, called the Ram Lila. On the final night, a huge straw statue of Ravana, filled with fireworks, is set alight with an enormous bang.

Dassehra is also called **Durga** Puja. Some Hindus worship Durga, a very fierce goddess who rides on a lion. People visit the **mandir** to offer flowers and food to an **image** of Durga. At the end of the festival, the image is paraded through the town then thrown into a river.

You make offerings to Durga in return for her blessing.

Putting on a play

Try putting on your own Ram Lila play at school or with some friends. The main characters are Rama, Sita, Ravana, and **Hanuman**, the monkey god who is Rama's faithful friend.

Hallowe'en

The 31 October is Hallowe'en, the night before the ancient **Christian** festival of All Hallows' or All Saints' Day. It was the night on which people thought that the ghosts of the dead came back to haunt them. Bonfires and lanterns were lit to frighten away any evil **spirits**.

Dressing up for a spooky Hallowe'en party.

At Hallowe'en parties today, people dress up as ghosts, witches or wizards, or wear spooky masks. They also play games, such as trick or treat. This is when children knock on doors and play tricks on adults who do not give them a treat. This custom started in ancient times to keep the Hallowe'en spirits happy. If you treated them well, they would leave you alone. But if you upset them, they might play all sorts of tricks on you!

Make a Hallowe'en lantern

Ask an adult to help you. To make a lantern, slice the top off a pumpkin and scoop out the insides. Then cut some triangles for the eyes and nose, and a grinning mouth full of jagged teeth. Put a night-light or candle inside. Then watch its ghostly glow!

All Saints' and All Souls'

On 1 November, the day after Hallowe'en, **Christians** celebrate All Hallows' or All Saints' Day. This is when they say thank you for the lives and work of all the **saints**. Many Christians mark the day by going to **church**. The word 'Hallowe'en' means on the eve or night before All Hallows.

The 2 November is All Souls' Day. On this day, Christians remember people who have died and say prayers for them so that their **souls** may go to heaven to be with God.

This church window shows an image of St Anne. She was **Jesus**'s grandmother. With her is Mary, Jesus's mother.

Kathina

The **Buddhist** festival of Kathina happens in October or November. In Asia, where most Buddhists live, this marks the end of the rainy season. While it rained, the **monks** had to shelter in **viharas**. They could not travel about to teach. They spent their time praying and **meditating**.

At Kathina, Buddhists visit their local vihara to take gifts for the monks and to thank them for all their hard work and help. They also bring new robes for the monks.

Buddhist monks in Thailand.

Saffron robes

Many Buddhist monks wear robes of a deep orange colour, called saffron. This is because many of the first monks lived in the forests. They found that this colour went well with the nature around them and did not frighten the animals.

Bonfire Night

'Remember, remember, the fifth of November,
With gunpowder, treason and plot.
I see no reason why gunpowder treason
Should ever be forgot!'

Every year, on 5 November, people celebrate Bonfire Night with firework displays and blazing bonfires. It remembers an event which happened almost 400 years ago, on 5 November 1605. This was when a man called Guy Fawkes and a group of plotters tried to kill King James by blowing up the **Houses of Parliament** in London. The plot failed and Guy Fawkes was executed (put to death). But the king ordered that the date should be marked every year as a warning!

Watching a blazing bonfire.

On Bonfire Night, people make a figure, or Guy, out of old clothes stuffed with paper or straw and burn it on top of a bonfire. It is a reminder of Guy Fawkes. The fireworks are a reminder of the gunpowder Guy Fawkes had hidden in the cellar of Parliament.

Penny for the Guy!

Fireworks lighting up the sky.

Guy Fawkes

*Bonfire Night is based on a true story. Guy Fawkes and the other plotters were **Catholics** who wanted to get rid of the **Protestant** king.*

Divali

Dates

19 October 1998
7 November 1999
26 October 2000
14 November 200

Later dates not known

In October or November, **Hindus** celebrate the festival of Divali. This is a very happy time in the Hindu year when people decorate their homes with small lights, called divas. They visit the **mandir**, exchange cards and gifts, and enjoy special meals.

Twinkling diva lamps for Divali.

There are many reasons for celebrating Divali. It remembers the joyful time when the god **Rama** came home to be crowned king. It is also a time for worshipping **Lakshmi**, the goddess of wealth and good fortune. Divas are lit to guide Rama back and to welcome Lakshmi into people's homes to give her blessing.

Visiting the mandir at Divali.

In India, Divali lasts for five days. In Britain, Hindus celebrate on the nearest weekend. Divali is also an important festival for **Sikhs**. They remember it as the time when **Guru Har Gobind** was freed from prison. He had been put there by the Indian **emperor**. People lit lamps to welcome him home.

New Year patterns

For some Hindus, Divali marks the start of the new year. To celebrate, they decorate the doorsteps of homes and mandirs with special rangoli patterns. These are symbols of welcome. Try drawing some of your own.

Remembrance Sunday

On a Sunday in November, people remember the millions of soldiers who died in the two World Wars (1914–1918 and 1939–1945) and in other wars. This is called Remembrance Sunday. It is held on the Sunday nearest to Armistice Day. This was the day on which the First World War ended on 11 November 1918.

To mark this solemn day, people lay **wreaths** of poppies by monuments remembering those who died. They also wear paper poppies. These stand for the poppies which bloomed in the fields in Belgium where the worst battles of the First World War took place.

The **Jewish** Remembrance Sunday is a week later.

Poppy wreaths are laid on Remembrance Sunday.

St Andrew's Day

On 30 November, Scottish people celebrate St Andrew's Day. St Andrew is the **patron saint** of Scotland. They mark the day with a special dinner, singing and Scottish dancing.

St Andrew's Cathedral in Scotland.

St Andrew was one of **Jesus**'s first **disciples**. He was later killed for his beliefs. According to legend, some of St Andrew's bones were brought to Scotland. They were placed in a **shrine** where St Andrew's **cathedral** now stands.

St Andrew's flag

St Andrew's **symbol** is a white X on a blue background. This is because St Andrew was **crucified** on an X-shaped cross. The blue stands for the sea. This is now the flag of Scotland.

27

Laylat-ul-Isra

Dates
15 November 1998
4 November 1999
24 October 2000
13 October 2001
2 October 2002

Laylat-ul-Isra is a **Muslim** festival. Its name means the Night of the Journey. It celebrates the journey **Prophet Muhammad (pbuh)** made from **Makkah** to **Jerusalem** on the back of a strange flying beast. He was taken up into heaven where **Allah** told him to teach Muslims to pray five times a day. Muslims celebrate this special night by reading the **Qur'an** and saying extra prayers.

The Dome of the Rock in Jerusalem. This is where Muhammad is said to have been taken up into heaven.

28

Guru Nanak's birthday

Every year, in November, **Sikhs** remember **Guru Nanak**'s birthday. Guru Nanak was the first Sikh **Guru**, or teacher. He was born in 1469. One day, he disappeared from his village. When he returned, he said that God had told him to teach people the right way to live. This is how the Sikh religion began.

An image of Guru Nanak.

To celebrate this happy day, Sikhs hold a special festival called a **Gurpurb**. They go to the **Gurdwara** to listen to talks and sing **hymns** about Guru Nanak's life. There is also a reading of their **holy** book, the Guru Granth Sahib, all the way through.

Glossary

Allah – Muslim word for God

ancestor – relation who lived a long time ago

atonement – making up for your wrongs

Buddhist – someone who follows the teachings of the Buddha, a great teacher who lived about 2500 years ago

Catholic – Christian who belongs to the Catholic Church

cathedral – important Christian church, where a bishop (senior priest) is based

Christian – person who follows the teachings of Jesus, who lived about 2000 years ago. Christians believe he was the son of God.

church – Christian place of worship

crucified – killed by being nailed to a wooden cross

disciple – follower of a religious leader or teacher

Durga – fierce Hindu goddess who rides on a lion or tiger. In her ten arms, she holds different weapons.

emperor – ruler of a country, like a king

fasting – going without anything to eat or drink

Ganesha – very popular Hindu god, shown with an elephant's head

Gurdwara – Sikh place of worship

Gurpurb – Sikh festival which celebrates the birth or death of one of the Gurus

Guru – Sikh teacher

Guru Har Gobind – Sikh leader who was put into prison for his beliefs

Guru Nanak – the first Sikh Guru. He taught people about how God wanted them to live.

Hanuman – the Hindu monkey god who helped Rama to rescue his wife, Sita

Hindu – follower of the Hindu religion, which began in India about 4500 years ago

holy – means respected because it is do with God

Houses of Parliament – huge, ancient building in London where the British government meets

hymn – song of worship

image – picture or statue of a god or goddess

Jerusalem – city in Jerusalem which is a holy place for Jews, Christians and Muslims

Jesus – religious teacher who lived about 2000 years ago. Christians believe that he was the son of God.

Jewish – to do with the Jewish religion

Jew – person who follows the Jewish religion which began in the Middle East more than 4000 years ago

Krishna – a very popular Hindu god, often shown with a blue skin and playing a flute

Lakshmi – Hindu goddess of beauty, wealth and good fortune

Makkah – city in the country we now call Saudi Arabia where the Prophet Muhammad (pbuh) was born. It is the Muslims' holiest place.

mandir – Hindu place of worship. Also called a temple.

meditating – thinking very hard about something important

monk – man who gives up his possessions and devotes his life to God. Buddhist monks devote their lives to the Buddha. Monks have to obey a strict set of rules.

Muhammad – the last great prophet of Islam. He was chosen by Allah to teach people how to live.

Muslim – someone who follows the religion of Islam

patron saint – saint who looks after a particular country or a particular group of people, such as travellers or doctors

pbuh – these letters stand for 'peace be upon him'. Muslims add these words after Muhammad's name and the names of the other prophets.

penitence – something you do to make up for your wrongs

prophet – person chosen by God to be his messenger

Protestant – Christian who belongs to the Protestant Church

Qur'an – Muslims' holy book

Rama – Hindu god whose story is told in the Ramayana

Ravana – wicked, ten-headed demon king who kidnaps Rama's wife, Sita

saint – person who has lived a very holy life

Shiva – one of the three most important Hindu gods. Shiva is the destroyer of the world.

shofar – Jewish musical instrument, made from a ram's horn

shrine – holy building or place

Sikh – Person who follows the Sikh religion which began in India about 500 years ago

soul – a person's spirit, which goes on living after they are dead

spirit – a being such as a ghost or fairy

symbol – sign with a special meaning

synagogue – Jewish place of worship

vihara – Buddhist monastery or place of worship

wreaths – flowers or leaves wound together into a ring or circle

Index